one-pot cooking

one-pot cooking

KYLE BOOKS

This edition published in 2004 by Kyle Books,
an imprint of Kyle Cathie Limited.
general.enquiries@kyle-cathie.com
www.kylecathie.com

Distributed by National Book Network
4501 Forbes Blvd., Suite 200
Lanham, MD 20706
Phone: (301) 459 3366
Fax: (301) 429 5746

ISBN 1-904920-06-3

Text © see page 176
Photographs © see page 176

The following are hereby identified as the authors of
this work in accordance with Section 77 of the
Copyright, Designs and Patents Act 1988: Darina
Allen, Hugo Arnold, Aliza Baron Cohen, Ed Baines,
Vatcharin Bhumichitr, Conrad Gallagher, Paul
Gayler, Adrian Mercuri, Oded Schwartz, Louisa J
Walters, Sarah Woodward.

The Library of Congress Cataloguing-in-Publication
Data is available on file.

Printed and bound in China by C & C Offset
Printing Co., Ltd.

contents

introduction

The basic principle behind each of the recipes in this book is simply that they can all be cooked using just one cooking pan or pot. It may be a casserole dish, or a skillet, a large saucepan, a baking sheet or a wok. Most kitchens, even those inhabited by the least keen cook, will have at least one of these items to hand. Some of the recipes make use of other material during the preparation, such as a mixing bowl, or a blender, but this material is kept to a minimum. Where it is used, there is usually time to wash it up before the final stage of cooking so that the cooking is finished with just one pot. Few home cooks have access to the huge battery of saucepans and skillets and gadgets that is available to the professional chef, and the recipes in this book reflect that reality. And of course, there's the question of the washing up – even if our cupboards are stuffed full of cutting edge kitchen equipment, that doesn't necessarily mean we want to get every single piece of it out every time we cook dinner, even if we do happen to own a dishwasher.

The nature of one-pot cooking implies recipes that are necessarily simpler than those that require a million pots and pans to make one dish. Simplicity doesn't have to mean blandness or dullness though. Many of these recipes are pared down to their vital ingredients, allowing the flavor and freshness of the ingredients to shine through. Layers of taste can be added throughout the course of the cooking to contribute to the final result.

This style of no-frills cooking suits today's busy lifestyle. Many of the recipes take half an hour or less to prepare, and of those that take longer, many can be left to their own devices to simmer or bubble away while you get on with something else.

One-pot doesn't have to mean one style of cooking either. There are recipes here for appetizers, soups, fish and shellfish, meat, side dishes and desserts. The recipes range

from simple salads to Thai curries, from silky soups to oven-braised vegetables and from stir-fries to kabobs. Many of them are quick enough to cook any night of the week and any of them you could serve to friends and family.

The same principles that apply to family eating can also be applied to entertaining. We no longer feel the need to spend hours on end slaving over a hot stove to impress our friends with the latest in food fashions. Today's entertaining is more relaxed and more about providing simple, fresh food to nourish our friends and family. Eating should be a pleasure, not a competitive sport.

One-pot cooking suits this style of entertaining. Many of the recipes presented here are complete meals in themselves and can even be carried to the table and served directly from the cooking pot. If you have cooked the dish in an attractive earthenware pot, or a handsome casserole dish, so much the better. Guests can tuck in and help themselves to seconds and thirds. In addition, the presence of just one pot on the table gets rid of the need for cramming two, three or four smaller dishes onto the table.

Most of us live in smaller spaces these days and few of us can fit a huge dining table into our kitchen or dining room (if we even have a dining room, that is). We are more likely to be round a small table in the corner of the living room. So the advantages of having just one pot on the table at dinner time are obvious, making the table less cluttered and the dining experience more pleasant.

There is a one-pot dish here for every occasion - dip in and find out which one you'll be cooking tonight!

tips & shortcuts

what sort of saucepans should I buy?

Buy the best quality heavy stainless steel pans that you can afford. Some pans have a 50-year guarantee – that should see you through a few home-cooked meals. The basics include: one large saucepan, one small saucepan, one skillet and one baking dish. If you have these, you can improvise most things. Other basic kitchen kit includes a mixing bowl, a measuring jug, a sharp knife and a wooden spoon.

get organised

Have all the ingredients ready before you start. If there are vegetables to be chopped, chop everything before you start. Wash up any bowls or cutlery you use as you go along, so at the end you are left with just the one pot and the plates and cutlery to wash up.

clean as you go

Sometimes you may be able to rinse out a pan you have used earlier in a recipe and use it later on as part of the same recipe. Aside from the obvious benefit of only using the one pan, it is also easier to clean them before food has a chance to solidify and attach itself to the pan. The sooner you do it, the quicker it is to do.

great gadgets

There are various gadgets to help with the principles of one-pot cooking. One of the best is the hand-held blender. This handy little gadget is great for blending soups and sauces directly in the pan, and some versions have a little bowl attached in which to chop small amounts of herbs, or to make mayonnaise. Not only does it save time, it also avoids yet more washing up - it is easy to rinse under running water when you have finished with it, and easy to store in a drawer, or on the wall.

how to use this book

Each recipe provides information about the number of servings it provides, and how long it takes to prepare and cook. As a general principle, the preparation time is the time it takes to wash, prepare, and chop the ingredients for the recipe, and the cooking time is the time you actually need to spend cooking, although for much of this time the dish may be able to be left to its own devices while you get on with something else.

In addition, each recipe provides nutritional information. As a rough guide, children, sedentary women, and older adults need approximately 1,600 calories per day. Teenage girls, active women, and sedentary men need 2,200 calories, and teenage boys, active men, and very active women need up to 2,800 per day.

There is information about the amount of fats per serving. Current advice is that no more than 10-30 per cent of our daily energy intake should come from fats. Most of us should be trying to cut down on total fats, particularly saturated fats.

Carbohydrates are given next - they are an important part of everyone's diet. It is recommended that at least a third of our daily intake is made up of starchy foods such as potatoes, yams, bread, pasta, noodles, chapattis, rice, sweet potatoes and so on.

It is recommended that our daily salt intake not exceed 6g. Most of us consume more like 9g (the equivalent of 2 teaspoonfuls). Much of the salt we consume comes from processed convenience foods, but approximately 10 per cent of it comes from salt we add to our food, either during cooking or at the table. High salt consumption is implicated in raised blood pressure, which is turn has been linked to a higher risk of heart disease and stroke.

appetizers

baked tomato & tapenade galette

4 x 6in rounds of puff pastry, 1/2in thick
4 tablespoons sun-dried tomato paste
8 medium plum tomatoes
4 tablespoons olive oil
selection of chopped fresh herbs, such as
    chives, parsley, chervil, and basil
4 tablespoons balsamic vinegar
salt and freshly-ground black pepper

Goat's cheese mixture
11/3 cups goat's cheese, chopped
1/3 cup heavy cream
2 tablespoons chopped basil
freshly-ground black pepper

Warm the goat's cheese and cream in a small saucepan and mix until well combined. Remove from the heat and add pepper and the chopped basil. Set aside.

Preheat the oven to 350°F. Place the puff pastry rounds between 2 sheets of waxed paper and place on a baking sheet. Lay another baking sheet on top (to ensure that the pastry won't rise), and bake for 15 minutes. Remove from the oven and allow to cool on a wire rack. Turn down the oven to a low temperature.

Spread the pastry rounds with the sun-dried tomato paste. Spoon a small amount of the goat's cheese mixture into the center of each round. Slice the plum tomatoes thinly and arrange on top. Drizzle the rounds with olive oil, season with salt and pepper and put in a low oven to warm for 3-4 minutes.

Serve sprinkled with fresh herbs, drizzled with balsamic vinegar.

TIP
Try using sliced zucchini instead of tomatoes, and arugula instead of mixed herbs - whatever takes your fancy.

Nutritional value per serving:
Calories: 720
Fats: 59.3g
Carbohydrates: 27g
Salt: 2.2g

roast beetroot with goat's cheese & balsamic vinegar

6-12 baby beetroot

4 tablespoons extra-virgin olive oil

4 large handfuls of arugula and beetroot leaves

1 tablespoon balsamic vinegar

3/4 cup goat's cheese

wild garlic leaves (if available)

sea salt and freshly cracked black pepper

Preheat the oven to 450°F.

Wrap the beetroot in aluminium foil and roast in the oven until soft and cooked through – between 1/2 and 1 hour, depending on size.

Rub the skins off the beetroot and keep whole or cut into quarters. Toss in half the extra-virgin olive oil. Scatter a few arugula and tiny beetroot leaves on each serving plate. Arrange a selection of warm beetroot on top. Drizzle with more olive oil and balsamic vinegar. Put 1 dessertspoonful of goat's cheese beside the beetroot. Sprinkle with sea salt and pepper and garnish with tiny beet greens or wild garlic flowers and serve.

TIP

If available, use a mixture of red, golden, and Clioggia beetroot

Nutritional value per serving:

Calories: 264

Fats: 22.3g

Carbohydrates: 6g

Salt: 1.13g

pomegranate, persimmon & pecan **salad**

3 ripe Fuyu persimmons (*Diospyros kaki* – little
    firm persimmons)

3 ripe pears (d'Anjou pears if you can find them)

1 lime, freshly squeezed

seeds from $1/2$ pomegranate

selection of lettuce, curly endive, watercress and
    arugula leaves

1 cup pecans, freshly toasted

Vinaigrette

2 tablespoons balsamic or sherry vinegar

2 teaspoons Dijon mustard

2 shallots, finely chopped

5 tablespoons extra-virgin olive oil

salt and freshly-ground black pepper

Preheat the oven to 350°F.

First make the vinaigrette: mix the vinegar, mustard, shallots, salt and pepper in a screw-top jar with the oil until emulsified.

Slice the persimmons and pears into slices about $1/2$in thick. Put into a bowl and sprinkle with the lime juice. Add the pomegranate seeds and toss gently.

Wash and dry the selection of leaves and store in a clean towel in the fridge until ready to use. Put the nuts onto a baking sheet in the oven for 5-6 minutes, tossing gently from time to time. Alternatively toast under a broiler.

When ready to serve: toss the leaves in some of the vinaigrette and arrange on eight plates. Toss the fruit mixture lightly in the remaining vinaigrette. Arrange on top of the greens and sprinkle with the toasted pecans. Serve immediately.

Nutritional value per serving:

Calories: 189

Fats: 13.7g

Carbohydrates: 16g

Salt: 0.23g

steamed mussels with garlic, cilantro & chile

2 tablespoons olive oil

4 cloves garlic, crushed

2 chiles, pitted and sliced

4 shallots, chopped

2in piece gingerroot, peeled and chopped

3 leeks, chopped

1 stick of celery, chopped

1 sprig thyme

1 sprig rosemary

2¼lb mussels, scrubbed and rinsed,
    with beards removed

1¼ cups white wine

4 cups fish broth

⅓ cup heavy cream

1 cup fresh cilantro leaves, chopped

1 cup fresh flat-leaf parsley, chopped

salt and freshly-ground black pepper

Heat the olive oil in a saucepan over low heat. Add the garlic, chiles, shallots, gingerroot, leeks, and celery. Cover and sweat for 5-6 minutes or until soft. Add the thyme and rosemary and transfer to a bowl. Rinse out the pan.

Place the mussels, white wine, and fish broth in the pan over high heat. Cover and steam for about 5 minutes, or until the mussels open. Remove the mussels with a slotted spoon and place in a serving dish, discarding any that have not opened.

Add the vegetables to the pan. Bring to a boil and cook until reduced by half. Remove from the heat, stir in the cream, and adjust the seasoning. Add the chopped herbs and pour over the mussels to serve.

How to chop fresh herbs

Wash and dry the herbs, discarding the stalks or saving them for the brothpot. Gather the herbs into a little ball and chop roughly. Change the angle of the knife to a horizontal position and rock the blade backwards and forwards until the herbs are chopped finely.

Nutritional value per serving:

Calories: 315

Fats: 19.8g

Carbohydrates: 9g

Salt: 1.7g

shrimp with ginger

2 tablespoons vegetable oil

2 garlic cloves, finely chopped

1in piece of fresh gingerroot, finely sliced

6-8 large raw shrimp, peeled and de-veined

1/4 teaspoon ground white pepper

1 tablespoon light soy sauce

1 tablespoon *nam pla* (Thai fish sauce)

1/2 teaspoon granulated sugar

2 tablespoons chicken broth or water

2 scallions, cut into 2in lengths

1 small onion, sliced

In a wok or skillet, heat the oil and fry the garlic until golden brown.

Stir in the gingerroot, then toss in the shrimp. Stirring after each addition, add the pepper, soy sauce, fish sauce, sugar and broth or water. Stir-fry together for about 2 minutes, then add the scallions and onion. Stir once, remove from the heat and turn on to a serving dish.

Nutritional value per serving:

Calories: 189

Fats: 11.7g

Carbohydrates: 6g

Salt: 3.13g

smoked fish with horseradish, wasabi, & mustard

4 teaspoons olive oil

4 slices of baguette, about 1/2in thick

3/4in piece of horseradish root

2 tablespoons sour cream

4oz smoked salmon

4oz smoked eel

3oz smoked cod's roe

scant 1 teaspoon wasabi paste

2 teaspoons good-quality Dijon mustard

freshly-ground black pepper

1 lemon, quartered, to serve

Preheat a hot broiler. Drizzle a teaspoon of olive oil over each slice of baguette and broil on both sides until golden brown. Set aside on wire rack.

Grate the horseradish and gently whisk it into the sour cream. Thinly slice the smoked salmon and cut the eel into 3/4in lengths (it looks more attractive if you do this at an angle).

Spread the cod's roe on the toasts and place these in the middle of 4 plates, then arrange the eel and salmon around them, together with neat piles of the horseradish cream, wasabi, and mustard. Sprinkle over a generous grinding of black pepper and serve with a lemon quarter.

Nutritional value per serving:

Calories: 243

Fats: 9.8g

Carbohydrates: 18g

Salt: 2.67g

carpaccio of **smoked salmon** with avocado, red onion, & dill

6-8oz smoked salmon

1-2 avocados

1 small red onion, finely diced

1 tablespoon chives, finely snipped

1 tablespoon fresh dill, finely chopped

1 tablespoon chervil or flat-leaf parsley sprigs

freshly cracked black pepper

Arrange the smoked salmon in a single layer on 4 large chilled plates. Peel and cut the avocado into $1/4$in dice. Sprinkle the salmon with the avocado and red onion dice. Garnish with snipped chives, chopped dill, and chervil or flat parsley sprigs.

Finally add a little freshly cracked pepper. Serve with crusty brown yeast bread.

TIP

Substitute very finely sliced blue or yellow fin tuna for the smoked salmon if you prefer.

Nutritional value per serving:

Calories: 136

Fats: 8.9g

Carbohydrates: 2g

Salt: 2.1g

tuna marinated in lime juice

14oz sushi-quality (i.e. extremely fresh) blue fin
   tuna, cut into ½in dice
juice of 3 limes
2 tablespoons olive oil
2 tablespoons tomato ketchup
few drops of Tabasco
½ ripe mango, peeled and cut into ¼in dice
¼ red bell pepper, cut into ¼in dice
½ avocado, peeled and cut into ¼in dice
1 red chile, pitted and finely chopped
2 scallions, roughly chopped
2 tablespoons roughly chopped cilantro
salt and freshly-ground black pepper

To serve
corn tortillas, cut into quarters and fried until
   crisp
lime wedges (optional)
cilantro leaves

Nutritional value per serving:
Calories: 275
Fats: 15.7g
Carbohydrates: 9g
Salt: 0.72g

Place the tuna in a bowl, pour over the lime juice, then add a little salt and leave for 30 minutes, until the tuna becomes opaque. Drain off the juice and combine some of it, according to taste, with the olive oil, tomato ketchup, and Tabasco to form a dressing.

Add the mango, red bell pepper, avocado, red chile, scallions, cilantro and some salt and pepper. Pour this dressing over the tuna, mix well, and chill for 1 hour.

Serve in cocktail-style glasses, garnished with the fried corn tortillas, lime wedges and cilantro leaves.

How to dice a mango

Cut off the 'cheeks' of the mango lengthways. Using the tip of a sharp knife, score the flesh in a criss-cross pattern. Turn the mango piece inside out and slice off the cubes close to the skin.

smoked chicken & avocado

1 whole smoked chicken
juice of 1/2 lemon
about 3/4 cup mayonnaise (preferably
   home-made)
3 firm, ripe avocados
1/2 cup hazelnut oil
1 tablespoon white wine vinegar
4oz bag mixed herb salad

Strip the chicken meat from the carcass and cut into small dice. Place in a bowl and add the lemon juice and enough of the mayonnaise to bind. Season to taste.

Halve, stone, peel, and slice each avocado as shown below.

Take a 2 1/2 in cooking ring and gently place on top of each portion of avocado. Fill with the smoked chicken mixture and carefully remove the mold. Place the hazelnut oil and white wine vinegar in a screw-top jar, season and shake until well combined. Place the salad leaves in a bowl, season and add enough of the dressing to coat, tossing lightly to combine. Arrange a small pile of dressed leaves on top of each salad and drizzle around a little more of the dressing to serve.

How to cut an avocado fan

Cut the avocado in half lengthways. Tap the stone sharply with the blade of a large knife and twist to remove the stone. Peel the avocado and slice, leaving the narrow end intact. Fan out the slices.

Nutritional value per serving:
Calories: 754
Fats: 71.4g
Carbohydrates: 2g
Salt: 3.63g

pancakes with pancetta & maple syrup

2 cups self-rising flour, sifted

1 teaspoon baking powder

2 tablespoons superfine sugar

pinch of salt

3 eggs

1 dessertspoon melted butter

$2/3$ cup full-fat milk

12 thin slices of pancetta

vegetable oil, for frying

maple syrup, to serve

In a mixing bowl, combine the flour, baking powder, sugar and salt. Whisk in the eggs, butter and just enough of the milk to form a batter about the same consistency as heavy cream (you probably won't need all the milk). Set aside.

Preheat a hot broiler and a low oven. Broil the pancetta until crisp and keep warm. Heat a skillet and, when hot, lightly oil it. Drop dollops of the pancake mixture into the pan so they make pancakes about $2^{1}/_{2}$in in diameter. You don't want them too thick, about $^{1}/_{2}$in, or they will not cook through. The pancakes will happily keep warm in the low oven until all are cooked.

When you have 20-24 pancakes, pile 5 or 6 in the middle of each of 4 warmed plates, top with the pancetta and pour over maple syrup. Serve with lots of coffee.

Nutritional value per serving:

Calories: 427

Fats: 18.9g

Carbohydrates: 51g

Salt: 2.01g

pan-fried wild mushrooms with parmesan & thyme butter

8oz wild mushrooms, wiped clean and stalks
    trimmed

2 tablespoons olive oil

knob of unsalted butter

1 tablespoon fresh thyme leaves

1 cup extra thick heavy cream

2 tablespoons snipped fresh chives

4 tablespoons Parmesan shavings

Cut the mushrooms into thin slices. Heat the oil in a skillet; when hot, add the mushrooms and sauté for 2-3 minutes or until golden brown and completely tender.

Add the butter and thyme to the pan and season to taste. Once the butter starts to melt, stir in the cream and chives. Cook for another 2-3 minutes until slightly reduced, stirring occasionally.

Divide the mushroom mixture among warmed wide-rimmed bowls and scatter the Parmesan shavings on top. Serve immediately with some crusty bread, if liked.

TIP

You can use ceps instead of wild mushrooms, but if ceps have been collected soon after rain they may exude a lot of moisture whilst cooking. If so, sauté until there is no more than a tablespoon of liquid remaining, then continue with the recipe.

Nutritional value per serving:

Calories: 336

Fats: 34.4g

Carbohydrates: 2g

Salt: 0.29g

aloo **chat**

½ cup ghee or clarified butter (see TIP)

1 small onion, finely chopped

8-10 (about 1lb) small waxy potatoes, peeled
and cut in half lengthways

1 small red chile, pitted and thinly sliced

1 teaspoon ground turmeric

2 teaspoons ground coriander

1 teaspoon cumin seeds, toasted briefly in a dry
skillet

²/₃ cup water

flesh from ½ small coconut, cut into shavings

fresh cilantro leaves, to garnish

salt

Heat the ghee or clarified butter in a skillet, add the onion and cook over a low heat until translucent. Add the potatoes, chile, turmeric, ground coriander, cumin seeds, and a little salt and fry for 10-15 minutes, until the potatoes are lightly browned. Add the water and bring to a boil. Reduce the heat to a simmer and cook gently until all the liquid has been absorbed and the potatoes are tender. Leave to cool, then arrange in a serving dish. Scatter over the coconut shavings and cilantro leaves before serving.

TIP

To clarify butter, heat gently in a small saucepan until it begins to boil, then boil for 2 minutes (or heat in a microwave for 1 minute). Pour through a fine conical strainer or a cheesecloth lined strainer, leaving behind the white, milky sediment. Store in the fridge.

How to shave a fresh coconut

Make two holes in the 'eyes' of the coconut using a screwdriver and hammer. Pour off the milk. Use the hammer to smash the coconut and prise the flesh off the shell. Shave small pieces of coconut off the chunks using a potato peeler.

Nutritional value per serving:

Calories: 433

Fats: 36.3g

Carbohydrates: 24g

Salt: 0.3g

soup

iced almond & garlic soup

1 cup blanched almonds

3 slices slightly stale country white bread,
   crusts removed

4 cloves garlic, preferably new season's

4 tablespoons fruity extra-virgin olive oil

4 cups iced water

2 tablespoons white wine vinegar

1 small bunch of white grapes, peeled, halved,
   and pitted

sea salt

Reserving four almonds, put the rest into the food processor along with the bread, garlic, olive oil, and half the water and process briefly. With the processor still on, keep adding water until you have the desired consistency – the soup should be smooth and not too thin. Add salt and vinegar to taste.

Chill for at least 1 hour – it should be ice cold when you serve it. Garnish each bowl of soup with an almond and a few grapes.

Nutritional value per serving:

Calories: 352

Fats: 28.9g

Carbohydrates: 15g

Salt: 0.56g

beetroot soup
with chive cream

8 medium beetroot

2 tablespoons butter

2 medium onions, chopped

5 cups hot chicken or vegetable broth

$1/2$ cup creamy milk

salt and freshly-ground pepper

Chive cream

125ml (4fl oz) sour cream or crème fraîche

small bunch chives, finely chopped

Wash the beetroot carefully under a cold tap. Do not scrub them – simply rub off the clay with your fingers. You do not want to damage the skin or cut off the tops or tails, otherwise the beetroot will 'bleed' while cooking. Put into cold water, bring to a boil and simmer, covered, for anything from 20 minutes to 2 hours depending on the size and age of your beetroots. They are cooked when their skins rub off easily. Remove these, and top and tail the beetroots.

When cooked, set the beetroot aside and rinse out the saucepan. Heat the butter and gently sweat the onions. Chop the cooked beetroot and add to the onions. Season with salt and pepper. Pour the hot broth into a blender with the vegetables, and blend until quite smooth. Reheat, add some creamy milk, taste and adjust the seasoning; it may be necessary to add a little more broth or creamy milk. Serve garnished with swirls of sour cream and a sprinkling of chives.

TIP

To serve the soup chilled, follow the recipe up the point where you season it. Blend, with just enough broth to cover, until smooth and silky. Season with salt and pepper. Fold in some cream and yogurt. Serve well chilled with little swirls of yogurt and finely chopped chives.

Nutritional value per serving:

Calories: 121

Fats: 6.5g

Carbohydrates: 13g

Salt: 1.03g

pea & mint soup with sour cream

2 shallots, chopped

1lb shelled fresh peas

2 tablespoons chopped fresh thyme

6 tablespoons single cream

2 tablespoons fresh mint leaves, finely
    shredded, plus a few whole leaves to garnish

2/3 cup sour cream

Bring 3 1/2 cups of water to a boil in a saucepan and then add the shallots, peas, thyme and single cream. Simmer gently for 8-10 minutes until the peas are completely tender and season to taste.

Purée the soup in batches in a food processor or with a hand-held blender, and then push through a fine strainer for a smoother, more velvety finish, if liked.

If serving warm, pour back into a clean pan, add the mint and season to taste. Reheat gently. Otherwise, just stir in the mint and chill for at least 2 hours. Ladle into wide-rimmed bowls and swirl the sour cream into each serving. Garnish with a few mint leaves and sprinkle with black pepper to serve.

TIP

Use frozen peas if fresh peas are not in season.

Nutritional value per serving:

Calories: 219

Fats: 13g

Carbohydrates: 17g

Salt: 0.07g

cauliflower & olive soup

1 medium cauliflower, cut into florets

3 tablespoons virgin olive oil

$1/2$ tablespoon unsalted butter

1 onion, chopped

1 small leek, white part only, chopped

$2^3/_4$ cups well-flavored chicken broth
(or vegetable broth)

$2/_3$ cup full-fat milk

6 tablespoons heavy cream

6 black olives, pitted, rinsed, dried off, and
very finely chopped

1 tablespoon chopped chives

salt and freshly-ground black pepper

Blanch the cauliflower florets in a large saucepan of boiling salted water for 2 minutes, then drain well. Rinse out the pan, and heat 1 tablespoon of the oil with the butter, add the onion and leek and sweat until tender. Pour in the broth and milk and bring to a boil.

Add the cauliflower, then reduce the heat and simmer for 15-20 minutes, until the cauliflower is almost puréed. Place in a blender or food processor and blitz until smooth. Return to the pan, add the heavy cream and olives and lightly season to taste - remember the olives are already salty.

To serve, pour into soup bowls, drizzle over the remaining olive oil and sprinkle over the chives.

Nutritional value per serving:

Calories: 283

Fats: 23.8g

Carbohydrates: 10g

Salt: 1.23g

coconut & curry soup

2 tablespoons olive oil

2 tablespoons freshly shredded gingerroot

2 tablespoons shallots, finely chopped

2 tablespoons red onion, finely chopped

2 tablespoons carrot, diced

2 tablespoons curry powder

2 x 14oz cans coconut milk

Heat the olive oil in a large saucepan. Add the gingerroot, shallots, red onion, and carrot and sauté for about 5 minutes until softened but not colored, stirring occasionally.

Add the curry powder to the pan and cook for another 2-3 minutes, stirring constantly. Pour in $1/4$ cup of water and bring to a boil, then add the coconut milk and just warm through.

Purée the soup with a hand-held blender in the pan and season to taste. Reheat gently, then ladle into warmed serving bowls and serve at once, garnished with a few shallot pieces.

TIP

Make sure you use a fresh, good-quality curry powder and not one that has been stuck in the back of the cupboard for the last six months!

Nutritional value per serving:

Calories: 395

Fats: 38.7g

Carbohydrates: 9g

Salt: 0.64g

chilled potato & watercress soup with caviar chantilly

2 bunches of watercress
1/2 stick unsalted butter
1 onion, chopped
2 leeks, white part only, chopped
4 medium floury potatoes, peeled and diced
3 1/2 cups chicken broth
1/2 cup heavy cream
salt and freshly-ground black pepper

For the caviar chantilly
1/3 cup heavy cream, semi-whipped
3/4 oz caviar

Pick the leaves from one bunch of watercress and set aside. Blanch the other bunch and the stalks in boiling water, then drain, refresh in cold water and drain again. Chop finely.

Heat the butter in a saucepan, add the onion, leeks and potatoes, then cover and sweat over a low heat until softened. Pour in the chicken broth, add the chopped watercress and bring to a boil. Simmer for 20-25 minutes, until the potatoes are falling apart. Puree the soup with a hand-held blender. Leave to cool, then stir in the heavy cream. Season to taste and chill thoroughly.

Pour into serving bowls, garnish with the reserved watercress leaves, then place a dollop of cream in the center of each portion and top it with the caviar.

Nutritional value per serving:
Calories: 457
Fats: 38g
Carbohydrates: 23g
Salt: 1.39g

andalusian fish soup with saffron aïoli

1/3 cup olive oil

1 onion, finely chopped

2 garlic cloves, crushed

1/2 teaspoon dried chile flakes

1 small bay leaf

1/2 teaspoon ground cumin

1 teaspoon shredded orange rind

good pinch of saffron strands

4 cups fish broth

11oz mixed shellfish (eg mussels and clams)

3 slices of white bread

1 teaspoon each tomato purée or passata and smoked paprika

1lb mixed firm white fish fillets cut into 1in pieces

salt and freshly-ground black pepper

Aïoli

1 garlic clove, chopped

A good pinch of saffron strands

1 tablespoon lemon juice

2/3 cup good-quality mayonnaise

Nutritional value per serving:

Calories: 703

Fats: 54g

Carbohydrates: 17g

Salt: 2.39g

Heat half the oil in a large ssaucepan, add the onion and cook for about 8 minutes, until tender. Add the garlic, chili flakes, bay leaf, cumin, orange rind and saffron. Pour in the fish broth, bring to a boil and simmer for 10-15 minutes.

Meanwhile, clean the mussels and clams under cold running water and pull out the beards from the mussels. Discard any open mussels or clams that don't close when tapped on the work surface.

Soak the bread in a little water, squeeze it dry, then place in a blender with the tomato purée or passata, smoked paprika, and the remaining oil. Process to a paste and add to the soup. Carefully add the fish to the soup and simmer gently for 5 minutes. Add the shellfish and cook for 3-4 minutes, until the shells open. Season to taste and keep warm. To make the aïoli, crush the garlic and saffron in a mortar with the lemon juice and then stir into the mayonnaise.

Divide the fish and shellfish between 4 serving bowls and pour over the broth. Serve with the aïoli, plus some good crusty bread to mop up the juices.

sauvignon blanc soup with smoked salmon

2 cups fish broth

1 cup light cream

1 cup Sauvignon blanc

5 egg yolks

good pinch of freshly grated nutmeg

4 smoked salmon slices

Place the fish broth in a heavy-based saucepan with the cream, Sauvignon blanc, egg yolks, and enough nutmeg to taste. Whisk until well combined, then bring to a gentle simmer and continue to cook, whisking continuously until the soup has slightly thickened and reached a soup-like consistency. Remove from the heat and season to taste.

Cut the salmon into strips and divide between four warmed wide-rimmed bowls. Ladle over the soup and add a sprinkling of black pepper and nutmeg to serve.

Nutritional value per serving:

Calories: 283

Fats: 20.2g

Carbohydrates: 3g

Salt: 1.72g

chickpea, bacon, & chile soup

3$^{1}/_{2}$ cups dried chickpeas/garbanzo beans

7oz piece of streaky bacon

3 tablespoons olive oil

1 large onion, finely chopped

2 garlic cloves, finely chopped

2 long red chiles, pitted and finely chopped

9 cups chicken broth (preferably home-made)

Place the chickpeas in a large bowl and cover with water. Set aside for 24 hours to soak. Drain the chickpeas and place them in a large saucepan with enough water to cover. Bring to a boil and boil vigorously for 10 minutes, then drain and rinse under cold water – this will eliminate any toxins that they may have. Remove the rind from the bacon and cut the piece in half, then cut half into strips and leave the rest in one whole piece; set aside.

Return the pan to the heat and add two tablespoons of the olive oil, then tip in the onion, garlic, and chile and sweat for about 5 minutes until slightly colored, stirring occasionally. Add the drained chickpeas and cook for another 2 minutes, stirring. Pour in the broth and add the whole piece of bacon, then bring to a boil. Reduce the heat and simmer gently until the chickpeas are tender – this can take anything from 1$^{1}/_{2}$-3 hours, depending on how old the chickpeas are.

Remove the piece of bacon from the chickpea mixture and discard, then puree the soup with a hand-held blender until completely smooth. Season to taste and keep warm. Heat a skillet and add the remaining olive oil. Tip in the reserved bacon strips and cook over a fairly high heat for 2-3 minutes or until golden brown. Drain on kitchen paper towels. Ladle the soup into warmed wide-rimmed bowls and scatter the bacon on top. Serve immediately.

Nutritional value per serving:

Calories: 729

Fats: 28.5g

Carbohydrates: 79g

Salt: 3.8g

TIP

Use canned chickpeas if you are short of time. Reduce the cooking time to approximately 30 minutes.

lebanese lentil soup

4 tablespoons olive oil

1 onion, finely chopped

1 garlic clove, crushed

1 cup red lentils

1 tablespoon freshly ground cardamom

$1/4$ teaspoon ground allspice

$1/2$ teaspoon shredded lemon rind

4 cups beef broth

2 tablespoons lemon juice

four small handfuls bread croutons

salt and freshly-ground black pepper

a few roughly crushed cardamom seeds,
    to garnish

Heat half the oil in a large saucepan, add the onion and garlic and cook for 2–3 minutes, until softened. Add the lentils and stir until coated in the oil. Add the cardamom, allspice, and lemon rind, then pour in the broth and bring to a boil. Reduce the heat and simmer for about 30 minutes, until the lentils are very tender. Cool slightly, then blitz to a coarse-textured purée with a hand-held blender. Reheat gently and season to taste. Stir the lemon juice and the remaining oil into the soup, add the bread croûtons, then garnish with the crushed cardamom and serve immediately.

Nutritional value per serving:

Calories: 336

Fats: 15.2g

Carbohydrates: 37g

Salt: 1.25g

corn bisque with cheese & smoked bacon

3 corn on the cob

1¼ cups full-fat milk

2 tablespoons unsalted butter

1 onion, chopped

1 celery stalk, chopped

1¼ cups all-purpose flour

¼ cup chicken or vegetable broth

1½ cups Cheddar cheese, grated

3oz piece of smoked bacon, thinly sliced

salt and freshly-ground black pepper

Remove the kernels from the corn as shown below. Put them in a saucepan with the milk and bring to a boil. Reduce the heat and simmer for 10-15 minutes, until tender. Drain the corn and reserve the milk. Rinse out the pan, then melt the butter and gently sauté the onion and celery until soft. Add the flour, cook for 2-3 minutes over a low heat and then gradually stir in the milk and broth. Slowly bring to a boil, stirring all the time, until thickened. Reduce the heat and simmer for 15-20 minutes. Add the corn and half the cheese and cook gently for 5 minutes, then blitz to a purée with a hand-held blender. Reheat and season to taste.

Grill the bacon slices until crisp, then crumble them. Sprinkle the bacon over the soup with the remaining cheese just before serving.

How to cut kernels off corn cobs

Remove the husks and the silky threads from the corn cobs. Hold each cob upright on a work surface and cut off the kernels with a sharp knife.

Nutritional value per serving:

Calories: 387

Fats: 25.4g

Carbohydrates: 22g

Salt: 1.99g

golden **pearl** barley soup

2$^1/_2$ cups vegetable broth

1 onion, finely chopped

1 stick celery, finely chopped

3 tablespoons pearl barley

pinch of saffron

pinch of mixed herbs

2oz rutabaga or yellow turnip

1 carrot, chopped

dash of soy sauce

handful of mung beansprouts

freshly-ground black pepper

Heat half of the vegetable broth in a large saucepan. Add the onion and celery and simmer for 5 minutes. Add the pearl barley, saffron, and mixed herbs and simmer for 30 minutes. Add the rutabaga, carrot and the rest of vegetable broth to the pan, cover and simmer for another 20 minutes, until the vegetables and barley are tender.

Add the soy sauce, pepper and beansprouts, simmer for 2-3 more minutes and serve.

Nutritional value per serving:

Calories: 254

Fats: 2g

Carbohydrates: 15g

Salt: 1.20g

moroccan carrot soup
with chermoula

2 tablespoons unsalted butter

1/2in piece of fresh gingerroot, very finely
    chopped

1/4 teaspoon ground turmeric

1/4 teaspoon ground cumin

1 onion, chopped

1 leek, white part only, chopped

8 medium carrots, cut into small chunks

1/4 teaspoon paprika

4 cups vegetable broth

salt and freshly-ground black pepper

Chermoula

2 cups fresh cilantro

1 garlic clove, crushed

1/4 teaspoon ground coriander

1/4 teaspoon ground cumin

1/3 cup olive oil

juice of 1/4 lemon

Heat the butter in a large saucepan, add the ginger, turmeric, and cumin and sweat for 1-2 minutes. Add the onion, leek, and carrots and sweat for 5 minutes. Stir in the paprika and then pour in the vegetable broth. Bring to a boil, then reduce the heat and simmer until the vegetables are tender, about 30 minutes. Purée with a hand-held blender until smooth, then reheat and season to taste.

For the chermoula, put all the ingredients in a blender and blitz to a smooth paste. Serve the soup in individual bowls, spooning about a tablespoon of chermoula over each portion.

TIP

Chermoula is the name given to a blend of herbs, spices, oil, and lemon juice normally used as a marinade for fish or meat. In this variation it is more of a sauce. It will make far more than you need but you can use it in all manner of ways - as a salad dressing, for pasta or as a vibrant, zesty side sauce. Chermoula will keep in the fridge for 3-4 days but will lose its bright color after 2 days.

Nutritional value per serving:

Calories: 328

Fats: 28.9g

Carbohydrates: 14g

Salt: 1.17g

spiced pumpkin soup

2lb pumpkin or winter squash, peeled, deseeded
  and cut into $1/2$in cubes
2 small onions, peeled and chopped
2 garlic cloves, crushed
2 tablespoons butter
1 sprig thyme
4 medium very ripe tomatoes, skinned and
  chopped, or 1 x 14oz can tomatoes, pitted
  and roughly chopped
1 tablespoon tomato purée or passata
5 cups well-flavored chicken broth
pinch of nutmeg
3 tablespoons butter
$1/2$ teaspoon cumin seeds
$1/2$ teaspoon coriander seeds
$1/2$ teaspoon black peppercorns
1 teaspoon white mustard seeds
2in piece of cinnamon stick
salt and freshly-ground pepper

Put the pumpkin or squash into a saucepan with the onion, garlic, butter, and thyme. Cover and sweat over a low heat for 10 minutes, stirring once or twice. Add the chopped tomatoes (plus $1/2$–1 teaspoon sugar if using canned tomatoes) and tomato purée, and cook until dissolved into a thick sauce. Stir in the broth, salt, pepper, and a little nutmeg and simmer until the squash is very tender. Discard the thyme stalk, then blend the soup with a hand-held blender. You may need to add a little more broth or water if the soup is too thick. Taste and adjust the seasoning.

Just before serving, gently reheat the soup and pour into a warm serving bowl. Heat the coriander, cumin, and peppercorns, and crush coarsely. Melt the butter in a small saucepan and, when foaming, add the crushed spices, mustard seeds, and cinnamon. Stir for a few seconds until the mustard seeds start to pop. Remove the cinnamon and quickly pour over the soup. Serve, mixing in the spiced butter as you ladle it out.

Nutritional value per serving:
Calories: 130
Fats: 9.3g
Carbohydrates: 9g
Salt: 1.05g

SERVES 6

PREPARATION TIME: 35 MINUTES

COOKING TIME: 25 MINUTES

potato & roasted red bell pepper soup

4 large red bell peppers, roasted and peeled as
   shown below
1/2 stick butter
4 medium potatoes, peeled and cut into
   1/2in cubes
1 medium onion, cut into 1cm (1/2in) cubes
1 teaspoon salt
freshly-ground pepper
1-2 tablespoons in total of the following:
   parsley, thyme, lemon, chives, all chopped
3 1/2 cups well-flavored chicken or vegetable
   broth
1/2 cup creamy milk
herbs, freshly chopped, and some chive or
   thyme flowers in season, to garnish

Purée the bell pepper flesh with the juices. Taste, season, and set aside. Melt the butter in a heavy saucepan. When it foams, add the potatoes and onions, and toss them in the butter until well coated. Sprinkle with salt and a few grinds of pepper. Cover with a butter wrapper or paper lid, and the lid of the saucepan. Sweat over a gentle heat for about 10 minutes. Meanwhile, bring the broth to a boil. When the vegetables are soft but not colored, add the broth, and continue to cook until the vegetables are soft. Purée the soup with a hand-held blender. Taste and adjust the seasoning. Thin with creamy milk to the required consistency. Just before serving swirl the red pepper purée through the soup or simply drizzle on top of each bowl. Top with some herbs and serve.

How to roast and peel bell peppers

Preheat the oven to 475°F. Put the bell peppers on a baking sheet and bake for 20-30 minutes until they are soft and blistered. Place in a bowl and cover with plastic wrap. Allow to cool. Peel the bell peppers and remove the seeds but do not wash them.

Nutritional value per serving:

Calories: 171

Fats: 8.3g

Carbohydrates: 21g

Salt: 1.51g

fish & shellfish

twice-baked potatoes with crabmeat & walnuts

4 baking potatoes, about 5oz each

⅓ cup sour cream

2 tablespoons chopped chives, parsley, or other
  fresh herbs

½ cup crabmeat

2 handfuls arugula leaves (half reserved for
  garnish)

fresh herb leaves, to garnish

chopped walnuts and chives, to serve

salt and freshly-ground black pepper

Preheat the oven to 350°F. Rinse the potatoes under cold water, wrap in aluminium foil and bake in the preheated oven for 1 hour. Remove from the oven and allow to cool completely. Leave the oven at the same temperature.

Cut off the top of each potato, leaving two thirds for the base. Scoop out the inside into a bowl, leaving a ¼in layer of potato attached to the skin. Add the sour cream, herbs, crabmeat, and arugula, roughly chopped, and mix well with the potato. Season to taste with salt and pepper. Fill each potato with some of the potato mixture. Place on a baking sheet and bake in the preheated oven for 20 minutes, or until golden brown on top. Garnish with fresh herbs and serve on a bed of chopped walnuts and chives.

Segmented crab

1lb of cooked crab in the shell yields about 6-8oz crab meat, depending on the time of year.

Nutritional value per serving:

Calories: 227

Fats: 9.5g

Carbohydrates: 28g

Salt: 0.61g

braised cod with navy beans, pearl onions, & red wine sauce

2 tablespoons olive oil

1/2 stick butter

2lb cod tails (or another firm white fish), trimmed

12 pearl onions, peeled

4 cloves garlic, crushed

4 large sprigs thyme

1 bottle of dark red wine

2 cups chicken broth

1 cup navy beans, soaked overnight

salt and freshly-ground black pepper

Preheat the oven to 350°F.

Heat a large casserole dish over moderate heat and add the olive oil and butter. Season the fish, add to the dish and cook for about 1 minute on all sides to seal. Remove the fish with a slotted spoon and set aside.

Add the pearl onions, garlic, and thyme and brown for a few minutes. Pour in the red wine and chicken broth. Drain the navy beans and add to the casserole. Cover and cook in the preheated oven for about 1 hour, or until the beans are tender.

Add the fish, cover and return to the oven for a further 10 minutes. Season to taste and serve immediately.

TIP

Use tinned navy beans if time is short, reducing the cooking time from 1 hour to 30 minutes.

Nutritional value per serving:

Calories: 664

Fats: 18.1g

Carbohydrates: 41g

Salt: 1.53g

cod curry with green mango & thai basil

2 tablespoons vegetable oil

2 tablespoons green curry paste

1lb cod fillet (or other firm white fish), cut into large dice

1 lemongrass stalk, hard outer layers removed, tender inner core chopped

1¼ cups coconut milk

4 kaffir lime leaves

1 teaspoon ground turmeric

1 teaspoon ground coriander

1 eggplant, cut into large batons

2 tablespoons *nam pla* (Thai fish sauce)

3 green chiles, finely sliced

½ green, unripe mango, peeled, pitted, thinly sliced

10 Thai basil leaves, roughly chopped

Heat the oil in a large heavy-based skillet, add the curry paste and fry until it bubbles and becomes fragrant. Add the fish and lemongrass and cook over a gentle heat for about 2 minutes. Stir in the coconut milk, kaffir lime leaves, turmeric and coriander and bring to a boil. Add the eggplant and fish sauce and cook over a gentle heat for about 5 minutes, until the fish is cooked. Finally stir in the green chiles and the mango. Serve immediately sprinkled with the basil.

TIP

If kaffir lime leaves are not available, replace them with a bay leaf and ½ teaspoon of shredded lime rindj.

Nutritional value per serving:

Calories: 302

Fats: 20.3g

Carbohydrates: 10g

Salt: 1.94g

soba noodles with soy, cilantro, & marinated squid

²/₃ cup olive oil

1 tablespoon butter

2 limes, sliced

1 stalk lemongrass, chopped

¹/₂ bunch of cilantro, chopped

¹/₂ cup chopped gingerroot

1lb baby squid, sliced in rings

2 cups soba noodles (available in Asian markets)

3 tablespoons soy sauce

2 tablespoons chopped cilantro

cilantro leaves, to garnish

Heat the olive oil and butter in a wok over gentle heat. Add the limes, lemongrass, cilantro and gingerroot and cook for 4 minutes. Remove from the heat and stir in the squid. Transfer to a shallow dish and leave to marinate overnight. Remove the squid from the marinade with a slotted spoon. Heat 2-3 tablespoons of the marinade in the wok, add the squid and stir-fry for 3-4 minutes.

Put the soba noodles in a large bowl and pour on enough boiling water to cover. Leave for 30 seconds, then drain and add to the squid. Mix well and add the soy sauce and cilantro. Serve immediately, garnished with cilantro leaves.

How to prepare squid

Cut off the tentacles then pull the entrails out of the sac and discard. Remove the 'beak' and pull the quill out of the sac. Pull off the wings and scrape the purplish membrane off them and the sac. Cut the body into rings.

Nutritional value per serving:

Calories: 378

Fats: 17.6g

Carbohydrates: 32g

Salt: 2.42g

SERVES 4

PREPARATION TIME: 20 MINUTES

COOKING TIME: 10 MINUTES

stir-fried **seafood** with garlic & peppercorns

2 tablespoons vegetable oil

3 garlic cloves, finely chopped

2½oz squid, cleaned and cut into ¾in pieces
  (see page 78)

4 raw king shrimp, shelled and de-veined

4 scallops

4 crab claws, bashed

1 tablespoon *nam pla* (Thai fish sauce)

1 tablespoon oyster sauce

1 tablespoon light soy sauce

½ teaspoon granulated sugar

½ teaspoon ground white pepper

2oz fresh green peppercorns, kept on their
  stalks and cooked in small bunches (available
  in Asian markets)

In a wok or skillet, heat the oil and fry the garlic until golden brown.

Add the seafood with the remaining ingredients and stir-fry over a high heat for 2-3 minutes. Transfer to a serving dish.

Nutritional value per serving:

Calories: 153

Fats: 8g

Carbohydrates: 2g

Salt: 1.63g

grilled **salmon** with vegetable salsa

4 heaped tablespoons fresh cilantro, chopped

1 red onion, finely chopped

4 plum tomatoes, peeled, pitted and diced
   (see page 90)

juice of 1 lemon

$\frac{1}{2}$ cup mayonnaise (preferably home-made)

1$\frac{1}{4}$lb fresh salmon fillet, skinned and
   thinly sliced

a little olive oil

To make the salsa; place half the cilantro in a bowl with the red onion, plum tomatoes and lemon juice, and season to taste. Mix to combine, then set aside for 30 minutes to allow the flavors to combine.

Preheat the broiler. Mix the remaining cilantro in a bowl with the mayonnaise and season to taste. Arrange the salmon slices on a large lightly oiled baking sheet so that they are overlapping.

Spread the cilantro mayonnaise on top of the salmon and broil for 30 seconds to 1 minute until the mayonnaise is bubbling and lightly golden and the salmon has just warmed through.

Carefully flake the fillets, combine with the salsa, and arrange on warmed serving plates. Serve at once with a mixed salad and some bread, if liked.

TIP

For an extra kick, add half a finely chopped red chile to the salsa.

Nutritional value per serving:

Calories: 502

Fats: 39g

Carbohydrates: 6g

Salt: 0.52g

grilled **sea bass** with chermoula

2 x 1½lb sea bass

Chermoula
2 cloves garlic
sea salt
2 teaspoon ground cumin
1 teaspoon paprika
¼ teaspoon cayenne pepper
3 tablespoons finely chopped fresh cilantro
1 tablespoon finely chopped fresh flat-leaf
   parsley
1 tablespoon finely chopped celery leaves
juice of half a lemon
half a preserved lemon, finely chopped
2 tablespoons olive oil

Mix together all the ingredients for the chermoula. Make several deep slashes across the flesh on either side of the fish. Spread the chermoula all over the fish, making sure plenty gets down into the slashes. Leave to marinate for 2 to 3 hours.

Preheat the broiler to maximum or better still get the barbecue coals glowing. Broil the fish close to the heat for 15 minutes on either side.

Nutritional value per serving:
Calories: 321
Fats: 12.5g
Carbohydrates: 2g
Salt: 0.71g

swordfish souvlaki with cumin

1lb 10oz swordfish fillet, trimmed and cut into
  1/2in cubes
2 tablespoons olive oil
2 tablespoons chopped parsley
1 tablespoon chopped oregano
1 teaspoon cumin seeds
pinch of smoked paprika
2 garlic cloves, crushed
juice of 1 lemon
1 red and 1 green bell pepper, cut into 1in dice
1 red onion, cut into small wedges

To serve
8 flatbreads, such as lavash (or even tortillas)
1/4 cucumber, pitted and chopped
2/3 cup Greek yogurt
2 tablespoons chopped mint
2 tablespoons chopped cilantro
1 garlic clove, crushed
salt and freshly-ground black pepper

Place the swordfish cubes in a bowl, add the olive oil, parsley, oregano, cumin seeds, paprika, and garlic and toss well together. Squeeze over the lemon juice and leave to marinate for 30 minutes.

Thread the swordfish on to 8 skewers, alternating it with the bell peppers and red onion, then brush with the marinade. Cook the souvlaki on a barbecue (or on a preheated ridged broiler pan if cooking indoors), turning them frequently and continually basting with the marinade; they will take about 4-5 minutes.

While the swordfish is cooking, wrap the bread in aluminium foil and warm it through in a moderate oven. Mix together the cucumber, Greek yogurt, herbs, and garlic and season to taste. Divide the mixture between the warm flatbreads, spreading it over the surface. Remove the fish from the skewers and place on the yogurt mixture, then roll up the bread into cones and serve immediately.

TIP
If you are using wooden skewers, soak them in water before using to prevent them from burning.

Nutritional value per serving:
Calories: 285
Fats: 13.5g
Carbohydrates: 8g
Salt: 0.60g

seared **scallops** with crispy pancetta & pea purée

7 tablespoons butter

2 shallots, roughly chopped

8oz fresh or frozen peas

1 teaspoon superfine sugar

2/3 cup double cream

juice of 1 lemon

12-20 scallops, depending on whether or not this is an appetizer or main course

8 thin slices pancetta

salt and freshly-ground black pepper

salad leaves, to serve

flat-leaf parsley, to garnish

Heat half the butter in a large skillet over gentle heat, add the shallots, cover and sweat until just starting to soften. Add the peas and cook for 1 minute before adding the sugar, seasoning and cream. Bring to a boil, then cook gently for about 15 minutes until the cream has reduced.

Purée the mixture with a hand-held blender and if the mixture is not thick enough cook gently until it has thickened slightly. Season with the lemon juice and transfer to a serving dish. Keep warm.

Rinse out the pan and heat the remaining butter on a high heat. Season the scallops well and sear on both sides for about 30-40 seconds. Add the pancetta and cook for another 1-2 minutes until the pancetta is crispy.

To serve, arrange the scallops on each plate with a slice of pancetta. Top with some salad leaves and another slice of pancetta, and finish with a spoonful of pea purée. Garnish with sprigs of flat-leaf parsley.

Nutritional value per serving:

Calories: 599

Fats: 45.8g

Carbohydrates: 10g

Salt: 2.26g

sizzling **shrimp** with sofrito, bell peppers, & manchego

4 tablespoons olive oil

1/2 stick unsalted butter

2 garlic cloves, crushed

20-24 large raw shrimp, shelled and de-veined

1 red onion, cut into wedges about 1/4 in thick

2 red bell peppers, halved, pitted and cut into
    strips 1/2in wide

1 green bell pepper, halved, pitted and cut into
    strips 1/2in wide

3 medium tomatoes, skinned, as shown, pitted,
    and chopped

pinch of cayenne pepper

1/2 teaspoon paprika

9oz Manchego cheese, cut into 1in cubes

2 tablespoons fresh cilantro leaves

salt and freshly-ground black pepper

Nutritional value per serving:

Calories: 593

Fats: 43.6g

Carbohydrates: 12g

Salt: 1.89g

Heat the oil and butter in a skillet until the butter is foaming, then add the garlic and cook for 1 minute. Throw in the shrimp and sauté them over a fairly high heat for about 1-2 minutes, until colored. Remove from the pan and keep warm. Add the onion and bell peppers to the pan, cover, and cook over a low heat for 15 minutes, until softened. Stir in the tomatoes, cayenne, and paprika and cook for about 5 minutes, until the tomatoes begin to break down. Return the shrimp to the pan, stir together, then add the Manchego and sauté for 30 seconds. Season to taste, scatter over the fresh cilantro and serve immediately.

TIP

Use feta if you can't get hold of the Spanish Manchego cheese.

How to skin and remove the skin from tomatoes

Cut a cross into the base of each tomato and plunge into a bowl of hot water. Leave for a few minutes until the skins start to wrinkle. The skins will then be easy to peel off.

meat

pork with cider apples in a **yellow curry** with shelled beans

4 tablespoons vegetable oil

2lb pork fillets, finely sliced into strips

3 shallots, sliced

1 stalk lemongrass, sliced

2 yellow bell peppers, pitted and finely sliced

1 tablespoon turmeric

1 tablespoon curry powder

2 Granny Smith or other tart apples, quartered
and cored

1¼ cups cider

2½ cups chicken broth

2lb fresh shelled beans, blanched until tender

1 tablespoon chopped cilantro

salt and freshly-ground black pepper

Heat half the vegetable oil in a preheated wok over high heat. Add the pork strips and sauté until golden brown in color. Remove the pork from the wok and keep warm.

Wipe out the wok with kitchen paper towels, then reheat with the remaining oil. Add the shallots, lemongrass, and bell peppers and sauté for 1 minute. Stir in the turmeric and curry power and cook for 1 minute. Add the apples and cook for 2-3 minutes.

Add the cider to the wok and simmer until reduced by half. Add the chicken broth and again simmer until reduced by half. Stir in the beans, pork, and chopped cilantro and season to taste. Serve immediately.

Nutritional value per serving:

Calories: 701

Fats: 30.5g

Carbohydrates: 33g

Salt: 1.16g

thai red pork & pumpkin curry

2 tablespoons olive oil

1lb lean pork, cut into 1in cubes

2 red chiles, pitted and finely chopped

2 tablespoons Thai red curry paste

2 x 6oz cartons coconut cream

1³/₄ cups chicken broth

1lb pumpkin, cut into 1in cubes

Heat a large saucepan. Add the olive oil and then tip in the pork and sear over a fairly high heat until lightly browned. Add the chiles and red curry paste and cook for 3-5 minutes, stirring with a wooden spatula.

Pour the coconut cream into the pan and mix to combine, scraping the bottom of the pan to remove any sediment. Add the chicken broth and pumpkin, then bring to a boil and reduce the heat. Simmer for 25-30 minutes or until the pumpkin is completely tender but still holding its shape and the sauce has slightly reduced. Season to taste and ladle into warmed wide-rimmed bowls to serve.

Nutritional value per serving:

Calories: 530

Fats: 42.2g

Carbohydrates: 8g

Salt: 0.85g

braised sausages with cauliflower & mustard

1lb) best pork sausages

4 tablespoons olive oil

2 onions, halved and thinly sliced into half-
    moon shapes

1 garlic clove, finely chopped

1 teaspoon fennel seeds

1 small cauliflower, broken into florets

3/4 cup chicken broth

1 dessertspoon Dijon or English mustard

salt and freshly-ground black pepper

Gently sauté the sausages in the olive oil until they are lightly colored. Add the onion and continue to cook for a further 10 minutes, taking care the onion doesn't burn. Add the garlic and fennel seeds, stir to coat in the oil and then stir in the cauliflower, stock and mustard. Season well with salt and pepper, cover and simmer for 10-15 minutes, or until the cauliflower is tender.

Nutritional value per serving:

Calories: 475

Fats: 35.9g

Carbohydrates: 17g

Salt: 2.98g

braised **lamb shank** with thyme, roast carrot, & pearl onions

2 tablespoons olive oil

4 lamb shanks, trimmed of excess fat and
   knuckle removed

2 medium carrots, peeled and cut into chunks

12 pearl onions, peeled

3 sprigs thyme

2 tablespoons water

2 tablespoons butter

1 tablespoon chopped flat-leaf parsley

1 tablespoon chopped thyme

salt and freshly-ground black pepper

Preheat the oven to 300°F.

Heat the oil in a large roasting pan on top of the stove. Brown the shanks on all sides, then remove from the pan. Add the carrots and onions and cook until golden brown, then remove from the tin.

Return the lamb shanks and any juices to the roasting pan with the thyme and water. Season with salt and pepper, then place in the oven and cook for 2 hours, turning occasionally. Return the carrots and onions to the pan and continue to cook for 1 hour.

Remove from the oven and transfer the lamb shanks and vegetables to warm plates. Remove the thyme sprigs. Skim off the fat from the juices in the roasting pan, then bring to a boil on top of the stove. Reduce for a few minutes until it has the consistency of a light sauce. Remove from the heat, add the butter and season to taste.

Spoon some sauce over each shank and garnish with flat-leaf parsley and thyme.

Nutritional value per serving:

Calories: 469

Fats: 31.5g

Carbohydrates: 6g

Salt: 0.74g

lamb & potato **hotpot**

8 middle-neck lamb chops

4 lamb's kidneys

2 tablespoons lard (or vegetable oil)

2 black puddings, cut into slices 1/4in thick

2 onions, thinly sliced

1 tablespoon thyme leaves

1 1/2lb baking potatoes, peeled and thinly sliced

3 cups hot meat broth

2 tablespoons unsalted butter

coarse salt and freshly-ground black pepper

Preheat the oven to 375°F. Trim excess fat from the lamb chops and remove the skin and central core from the kidneys.

Heat the lard in a heavy casserole, add the lamb chops and fry for 2-3 minutes, until well-sealed and golden on both sides. Remove and set aside. Add the kidneys and black pudding and seal them on both sides, then remove from the pan.

Add the onions and half the thyme to the casserole and fry for 4-5 minutes, until golden. Place the meat on top, starting with the lamb, then the kidneys and finally the black pudding. Arrange the potatoes in overlapping slices over the black pudding, seasoning with salt and pepper as you go. Sprinkle over the remaining thyme leaves.

Pour over the hot broth so that the potatoes are just covered, add a final seasoning, then dot the top of the potatoes with the butter. Cover the casserole, transfer to the oven and bake for 1-1 1/4 hours. Remove the lid and bake for a further 30 minutes to crisp up the potatoes and give them a lovely golden color.

How to prepare kidneys

Remove the fat (suet) from around the kidneys. Cut the kidneys in half lengthways and peel off the outer membrane. Remove the inner ducting from the kidneys using scissors.

Nutritional value per serving:

Calories: 739

Fats: 45.4g

Carbohydrates: 44g

Salt: 2.64g

roast pigeon with green olives, saffron, & preserved lemon

2 teaspoons hot paprika

2 teaspoons turmeric

2 teaspoons ground cumin

1/2 cup olive oil, plus 1 tablepoon

6 x 13oz pigeons

24 red shallots, peeled

2 tablespoons ghee or clarified butter

6 cloves garlic, crushed

2 teaspoons freshly shredded gingerroot

3 1/2oz pigeon livers

5 cups pigeon broth or chicken broth

12 large green olives, pitted and quartered

1 teaspoon saffron

1 preserved lemon, finely chopped

2 tablepoons lemon juice

1/2 teaspoon freshly-ground black pepper

3 tablespoons unsalted butter, diced

1 tablespoon chopped cilantro leaves.

Nutritional value per serving:

Calories: 547

Fats: 36.5g

Carbohydrates: 7g

Salt: 2.24g

Preheat the oven to 400°F. Mix half the paprika, turmeric and cumin with the olive oil. Brush the pigeons inside and out with the spiced olive oil.

Slice 12 shallots. Heat the ghee in a large heavy roasting pan over a moderate heat. Add the sliced shallots, garlic, gingerroot, and pigeon livers and fry for 2 minutes. Add the remaining paprika, turmeric, and cumin and cook for another 2 minutes. Pour in the broth and bring to a boil, then reduce the heat and simmer until the broth has reduced by half.

Strain the sauce through a fine strainer, return to the pan and bring to a boil. Add the remaining shallots and simmer for 15 minutes. Add the olives, saffron, and preserved lemon and simmer for another 5 minutes, then remove from the heat. Pour the sauce into a bowl and keep warm.

Add the tablespoon of oil to the roasting pan over a high heat. Add the pigeons and cook for 2-3 minutes, turning until seared on all sides. Transfer to the preheated oven and roast for 8 minutes. Remove the pigeons from the pan and keep warm.

Return the sauce to the pan to warm through. Whisk in the lemon juice, pepper and butter and stir in the cilantro leaves. Place a pigeon in the center of each plate and pour the sauce around the edge. Serve whole or cut in half.

whole roast quail stuffed with thyme, garlic, & lemon

6 quails
2 tablespoons Dijon mustard
3 teaspoons olive oil
redcurrant jelly, to serve (optional)

Stuffing
3 large pork sausages
grated rind of 2 lemons
a bunch of fresh thyme, leaves stripped from
    the stalks
1 garlic clove, mashed with a pinch of salt
5 teaspoons olive oil

Preheat the oven to 350°F. Make the stuffing: squeeze the sausage meat out of the skins and place in a bowl. Mix in the lemon rind, chopped thyme leaves, mashed garlic and olive oil. Blend all the stuffing ingredients together well, roll the mixture into 6 equally sized sausage shapes and stuff each quail with one.

Blend together the mustard and olive oil, and brush this mixture over the skin of each quail. Place the quails in a roasting pan and cook for 25–30 minutes. Remove and allow to cool. These quails serve wonderfully well with redcurrant jelly.

Nutritional value per serving:
Calories: 354
Fats: 25.8g
Carbohydrates: 3g
Salt: 1.16g

chicken **schnitzels** with mustard, capers, & lemon

4 boneless, skinless chicken breasts, flattened
    as shown below

1 large tablespoon Dijon mustard

3 tablespoons honey

juice and shredded rind of 1 lemon

4 tablespoons plain flour

2 eggs, beaten

2 cups fresh white breadcrumbs

2 tablespoons olive oil

1/2 stick unsalted butter

2 tablespoons superfine capers, drained and
    rinsed

1 tablespoon chopped parsley

2 lemons, peel and pith removed, cut into slices

salt and freshly-ground black pepper

Mix the mustard, honey, and lemon rind together in a bowl and then brush the mixture liberally all over the flattened chicken breasts. Season with salt and pepper. Dip the chicken in the flour to coat it, then in the beaten egg, and finally dredge it in the breadcrumbs.

Heat the oil in a large skillet, add the schnitzels and fry for about 2-3 minutes per side, until golden and cooked through. Add the butter to the pan and, when it begins to foam, add the capers, parsley and lemon juice. Spoon this mixture over the schnitzels, then transfer to 4 warm serving plates. Garnish with the lemon slices and serve immediately.

How to flatten chicken breasts

Place each chicken breast between 2 sheets of plastic wrap and, with a meat mallet or rolling pin, bash them out into escalopes about 1/2in thick.

Nutritional value per serving:

Calories: 558

Fats: 21.5g

Carbohydrates: 51g

Salt: 2.23g

marinated chicken with chopped shallots & garlic

1 chicken, jointed into 8 pieces

Marinade
2 tablespoons olive oil
2 tablespoons balsamic vinegar
bunch of thyme, chopped
2 tablespoons chopped shallots
4 unpeeled garlic cloves, smashed and roughly
    chopped
salt and freshly-ground black pepper

Well ahead, ideally the day before, put the chicken in a large bowl with the marinade ingredients and a generous grinding of black pepper. Toss so everything is well coated, cover and set aside for at least a few hours, preferably overnight.

Preheat the oven to 425°F.

Toss the chicken so it is well coated in the marinade, season with plenty of salt and place at the top of the oven. Turn gently twice while it is cooking (which should take about 30 minutes). Remove from the oven and allow to rest in a warm place for 15 minutes before serving.

Nutritional value per serving:
Calories: 357
Fats: 24.6g
Carbohydrates: 1g
Salt: 0.55g

tagine of chicken with preserved lemon

2½-3½lb chicken

3 cloves garlic, peeled and crushed

1 teaspoon coarse sea salt

1 small bunch fresh cilantro, very finely chopped

juice of half a lemon

1 large white onion, peeled and shredded

1 teaspoon freshly-ground black pepper

½ teaspoon saffron filaments

4 tablespoons olive oil

1 stick cinnamon

2 preserved lemons

1¾ cups green cracked olives

Rub the garlic, salt, lemon juice, and the cilantro into the cavity of the chicken. Mix together the onion, spices, and olive oil and rub over the outside of the chicken. Leave to stand for 30 minutes.

Place the chicken breast-side down in a tagine or heavy oval casserole, making sure you add all the marinade juices. Pour in sufficient water to cover two thirds of the chicken and add the stick of cinnamon. Bring the water to a boil, then reduce to a simmer and cook for 1 hour, turning the chicken several times during cooking. Preheat the oven to 300°F.

Rinse the preserved lemons and olives under cold running water. Cut the preserved lemons into strips. Remove the chicken from the casserole if that is what you are using, place in an earthenware serving dish and cover with aluminium foil to keep warm (if you have a tagine, drain the sauce into a pan). Turn up the heat under the casserole for 5 minutes to reduce the sauce. Pour the sauce over the chicken in the tagine and add the olives and preserved lemons. Place in the oven for 10 minutes then serve.

Nutritional value per serving:

Calories: 618

Fats: 45.5g

Carbohydrates: 7g

Salt: 4.17g

lemongrass soy chicken skewers

4 skinless, boneless chicken breasts, cut into
   1in cubes
8 lemongrass stalks, outer layers removed

Marinade
1 tablespoon honey or maple syrup
4 garlic cloves, crushed
1in piece of fresh gingerroot, finely chopped
2 green chiles, finely chopped
juice of 2 limes
shredded rind of 1 lime
4 tablespoons rice wine vinegar
2 tablespoons sweet chili sauce
4 tablespoons dark soy sauce, plus extra to
   serve
pinch of turmeric

Place all the marinade ingredients in a bowl and mix together well. Add the chicken, then cover and leave to marinate in the fridge for at least 8 hours – preferably 2 days for the best flavor.

Remove the chicken cubes from the marinade and thread them on to the 8 lemongrass stalks. Heat a barbecue, ideally, or a ridged broiler pan until smoking. Add the skewers and cook for 8-10 minutes, turning them regularly and brushing liberally with the marinade. Serve hot from the grill, with some extra soy sauce for dipping.

Nutritional value per serving:
Calories: 162
Fats: 1.6g
Carbohydrates: 3g
Salt: 1.29g

minted chicken & eggplant **salad**

sesame oil, for frying

4 skinless, boneless chicken breasts

1 eggplant, cut into slices ½in thick

2 tablespoons brown sugar

1 tablespoon *nam pla* (Thai fish sauce)

1 garlic clove, crushed

2 green chiles, thinly sliced

juice of 4 limes

1 lemongrass stalk, outer layers removed,
     tender inner core very finely chopped

1 onion, thinly sliced

2 shallots, chopped

1 cup mint leaves

4 tablespoons roasted peanuts, chopped

salt and freshly-ground black pepper

Cook the chicken breasts as shown below. Brush the eggplant slices with sesame oil, place on the broiler and cook until lightly charred, turning them regularly.

Meanwhile, place the sugar in a bowl, add the fish sauce, garlic, chiles and lime juice and mix well. Stir in the lemongrass, onion, and shallots.

Remove the chicken and eggplant from the broiler and leave to cool, then tear the chicken and cut the eggplant into small dice. Add to the bowl, toss well, cover with plastic wrap and leave to marinate at room temperature for 1 hour. Add the mint leaves and serve in a deep bowl, sprinkled with the peanuts.

How to panbroil chicken breasts

Heat a ridged broiler pan. Brush each chicken breast (not the pan) with a little sesame oil, then season the chicken breasts and place on the pan. Cook for 5-6 minutes on each side, until lightly charred and cooked through.

Nutritional value per serving:

Calories: 304

Fats: 10.1g

Carbohydrates: 15g

Salt: 1.31g

thai green curry with baby eggplants & sticky rice

2 stalks lemongrass

½in gingerroot

1 clove garlic

½ chile, pitted

½ lime

1 chicken, cut into 6 joints

3 tablespoons olive oil

1 cup chicken broth

4 lime leaves

2in piece of fresh galangal

½ cup coconut milk

2 tablespoons Thai green curry paste

2 tablespoons *nam pla* (Thai fish sauce)

⅔ cup coconut cream

1 tablespoon chopped cilantro

juice of ½ lime

8 baby eggplants, halved

4 tablespoons olive oil

salt and freshly-ground black pepper

First make a lime broth. Place the lemongrass, gingerroot, garlic, chile, and lime in a casserole and simmer for 15 minutes. Bring to a boil and boil until reduced by a quarter. Strain the broth and rinse the casserole.

Season the chicken pieces with salt and pepper. Heat the olive oil in a large casserole dish and brown the chicken over a medium heat. Cover the pan, reduce the heat and cook for 25 minutes, turning the chicken pieces occasionally.

Meanwhile, prepare the baby eggplants. Preheat a broiler or griddle pan. Rub the eggplants with olive oil and salt and broil for 5 minutes on each side, until tender.

Place the chicken broth, lime leaves, and galangal in a large saucepan. Bring to a boil, then remove from the heat and leave to infuse for 15 minutes. Strain the broth and return to the pan. Add the lime broth and boil vigorously for about 15 minutes, or until reduced by half. Stir in the coconut milk, curry paste, fish sauce and coconut cream then add the chicken pieces. Sprinkle with the chopped cilantro and lime juice.

Serve with the baby eggplants and some sticky rice.

Nutritional value per serving:

Calories: 742

Fats: 62.1g

Carbohydrates: 7g

Salt: 3.35g

TIP

The baby eggplants here are charbroiled for a more dramatic presentation, but they could be cooked in the casserole with the chicken, if preferred.

cassoulet

5½ cups haricot beans

1 carrot

1 onion studded with 2 cloves

2 x bouquet garni

8oz streaky bacon or pickled pork

3 tablespoons olive oil

3 onions, sliced

5 garlic cloves, crushed

6-8 very ripe tomatoes, peeled and sliced

5 cups chicken broth

4 legs of confit de canard (duck) or 2 pieces of
    confit d'oie (goose) or 4 fresh duck legs

1lb shoulder of lamb, cut into 4 thick chops

¾-1lb coarse pork sausages

½ cup breadcrumbs

salt and freshly-ground pepper

parsley, chopped

Nutritional value per serving:

Calories: 893g

Fats: 51.2g

Carbohydrates: 59g

Salt: 3.11g

Preheat the oven to 300°F.

Soak the beans overnight in plenty of cold water. Next day cover with fresh water, add the carrot, the clove-studded onion and one of the bouquet garni. Cover and cook for ½-¾ hour or until the beans are three-quarters cooked. Drain and discard the vegetables and bouquet garni.

Meanwhile, cut the bacon into 1in squares. Heat the olive oil in a casserole, add the bacon and fry until beginning to turn golden, add the onions, garlic, tomatoes, salt, pepper and a new bouquet garni. Cook for 1-2 minutes, add the broth and allow to simmer for 15 minutes.

Discard the bouquet garni, then add the duck or goose confit, lamb, sausage and finally put the beans on top. Bring the cassoulet to a boil, then spread a layer of breadcrumbs over the top. Put the pot into the slow oven, and continue to cook for 1-1½ hour or so until the beans and meat are fully cooked. By this time a crust will have formed and the beans will have absorbed most of the broth; if they haven't, remove the lid from the saucepan and cook uncovered for a further 15 minutes or so.

Sprinkle with chopped parsley and serve from the casserole (if you have cooked it in an earthenware pot all the better). Serve with a good green salad.

hungarian beef goulash

7 tablespoons butter

2lb beef, cut into cubes

4 medium onions, chopped

4 tablespoons paprika

1/2 cup all-purpose flour

1 tablespoon tomato purée or passata

2 quarts beef broth

4 medium carrots, peeled and cut into chunks

4 medium potatoes, peeled and cut into chunks

chopped parsley, to garnish

salt and freshly-ground black pepper

Preheat the oven to 400°F. Heat the butter in a large, heavy casserole, season the beef and add to the dish. Add the onions and cook for 2 minutes, stirring. Add the paprika and flour, mix well and place in the preheated oven, uncovered, for 10 minutes. Remove from the oven and mix in the tomato purée. Reduce the oven temperature to 350°F. Add enough of the broth to cover the meat. Bring to a boil on top of the stove and season. Cover with a lid and return to the oven for 2 hours. After 1 1/2 hours, mix in the chopped carrots and potatoes and cook for another 30 minutes, or until the meat and vegetables are tender. Sprinkle with chopped parsley to serve.

How to chop an onion

Cut the onion in half from top to bottom. Peel the skin, leaving the root intact. With half an onion cut-side down, make horizontal cuts towards the root, then cut the onion lengthways. Finally cut the onion crossways into dice.

Nutritional value per serving:

Calories: 546

Fats: 28.4g

Carbohydrates: 32g

Salt: 1.95g

marinated **steak** skewers

1 onion, thinly sliced

4in piece fresh gingerroot, peeled and cut into
    fine matchsticks

$1/2$ cup dark soy sauce

1lb steak, cut into 1in cubes

4 tablespoons olive oil

4oz shiitake mushrooms, sliced

2 carrots, peeled and shredded

Place the onion, gingerroot and soy sauce in a shallow non-metallic dish. Add the steak cubes, stirring to combine, then cover with plastic wrap and chill for at least 3 hours or overnight.

Heat a large non-stick skillet until hot. Drain the beef from the marinade, reserving it to use later, then thread the beef on to 8 x 6in wooden skewers. Add the oil to the pan and when the oil begins to smoke, sear the skewers on all sides – you may have to do this in two batches, depending on the size of your pan. Transfer to a warmed plate and keep warm.

Add the mushrooms and carrots to the same pan that you have cooked the beef in, then sauté for 2 minutes. Add four tablespoons of the reserved marinade, reduce the heat and continue to cook for about 1 minute, stirring occasionally. Arrange the skewers on warmed serving plates with the vegetables and spoon over any remaining sauce. Serve at once.

Nutritional value per serving:

Calories: 350

Fats: 21.2g

Carbohydrates: 12g

Salt: 5.93g

hamburgers with avocado sauce

1 tablespoon butter

1 small onion, finely chopped

1lb beef, freshly ground

$^1/_2$ teaspoon fresh thyme leaves

$^1/_2$ teaspoon parsley, finely chopped

1 small egg, beaten

salt and freshly-ground black pepper

pork caul fat (optional)

Avocado sauce

2 ripe avocados

3-4 tablespoons lime or lemon juice

1 tablespoon olive oil

1 tablespoon fresh cilantro or flat leaf parsley

sea salt and freshly-ground pepper

Melt the butter in a saucepan and toss in the onion, sweating until soft but not colored. Leave to get cold. Meanwhile mix the ground beef with the herbs and beaten egg, season with salt and pepper, add the onions and mix well. Shape into 8 hamburgers. Wrap each in caul fat if using. Cook to your taste in a medium-hot pan or on the barbecue for approximately 5-8 minutes on each side, turning once.

To make the avocado sauce, scoop out the flesh from the avocados and mash with a fork. Add the lime juice, olive oil, cilantro, salt and pepper to taste. Serve with the hamburgers.

How to wrap burgers in caul fat

Unravel the caul fat - you may have to dip it in a bowl of cold water to do this. Wrap each burger loosely to allow for contraction during cooking.

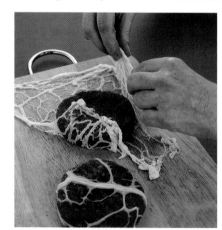

Nutritional value per serving:

Calories: 201

Fats: 15.6g

Carbohydrates: 1g

Salt: 0.43g

pappardelle with **rabbit** loin, mustard, & parsley

110g (4oz) dried pappardelle or wide flat
 noodles
1/2 stick butter
8 rabbit loins
2 shallots, diced
1 clove garlic, diced
10 oyster mushrooms
2/3 cup white wine
1 1/4 cups chicken broth
1 tablespoon wholegrain mustard
1 tablespoon heavy cream
1 tablespoon chopped flat-leaf parsley
10-12 blanched spinach leaves (optional)
salt and freshly-ground black pepper

Cook the pappardelle in a large sauté pan of boiling salted water until al dente. Drain and reserve. Rinse out the pan.

Heat half the butter in the pan over moderate heat. Season the rabbit and sauté for about 10 minutes on each side, or until cooked through, then remove from the pan and keep warm.

Add the remaining butter to the pan and sauté the shallots, garlic, and oyster mushrooms for 2 minutes. Add the white wine and bring to a boil, reducing the mixture by half, then add the broth and reduce again. Add the rabbit, mustard and cream and mix in the pappardelle. Allow to simmer for 3 minutes, until the pasta is heated through. Add the chopped parsley and season to taste.

For an optional presentation, as shown here, take half the cooked rabbit and cut into medallions. Wrap the rabbit pieces in blanched spinach leaves, return to the pan and warm through.

Nutritional value per serving:
Calories: 530
Fats: 24.1g
Carbohydrates: 25g
Salt: 1.30g

orzo with feta, mint, & plum tomatoes

2 cups orzo pasta shapes

4 tablepoons extra virgin olive oil

juice of 2 lemons

2 tablespoons finely chopped mint

1$\frac{1}{3}$ cups feta cheese, diced

4 plum tomatoes, finely diced

1 cup good quality stoned black olives

mint or arugula leaves and sun-dried tomatoes,
    to garnish

salt and freshly-ground black pepper

Cook the orzo in boiling salted water until al dente, then drain, rinse under cold water, and drain again thoroughly.

Mix in the remaining ingredients, season well and serve garnished with mint or arugula leaves and sun-dried tomatoes.

TIP

Orzo are small pasta shapes which look like grains of rice.

Nutritional value per serving:

Calories: 507

Fats: 27.4g

Carbohydrates: 52g

Salt: 3.64g

vegetable
side
dishes

roast new **potatoes** with rock salt & rosemary

24 (about 1½lb) baby new potatoes
⅓ cup olive oil
3 teaspoons rock salt
5 sprigs rosemary
2 cloves garlic, crushed
½ stick butter
freshly-ground black pepper

Preheat the oven to 350°F. Place the potatoes in a large roasting pan, drizzle with the olive oil and sprinkle with 2 teaspoons of the salt and the pepper. Bake in the preheated oven for about 30 minutes, or until the potatoes are golden brown and starting to shrivel slightly.

Add the rosemary, garlic, and butter. Shake the roasting tin and bake for another 10 minutes. These potatoes can be served hot or warm, sprinkled with the remaining salt.

Nutritional value per serving:
Calories: 386
Fats: 28.3g
Carbohydrates: 31g
Salt: 0.30g

curried shoestring potatoes

8 large (about 2lb) large potatoes

3-4 tablepoons curry powder

4 garlic cloves, peeled and sliced

2 tablespoons of garlic mayonnaise

Heat the vegetable oil to 375°F in an electric deep-fat fryer or large saucepan (use a cooking thermometer if necessary).

While the oil is heating, prepare the potatoes. Peel the potatoes and using a mandolin, cut them into long, thin strips so they resemble shoestrings (fine julienne).

Place the potatoes in a large bowl and sprinkle over the curry powder and add the sliced garlic, tossing to combine. Set aside for 3-5 minutes until the starch begins to leak from the potatoes and the mixture starts to look sticky.

Deep fry the potatoes for 3-4 minutes until golden brown (discarding the sliced garlic). Drain on plenty of kitchen paper towels and season to taste. Pile them into newspaper cones that are set on warmed serving plates, drizzle over the garlic mayonnaise and serve at once.

Nutritional value per serving:

Calories: 463

Fats: 35.4g

Carbohydrates: 33g

Salt: 0.19g

boiled potatoes with hot paprika & almond dressing

16 (about 2lb) new potatoes

Dressing
1 garlic clove, chopped
$1/3$ cup whole blanched almonds
$1/4$ teaspoon cayenne pepper
$1/4$ teaspoon hot paprika (or chili powder)
1 tablespoon sherry vinegar
4 tablespoons olive oil
1 tablespoon chopped parsley
1 tablespoon chopped oregano
salt

Boil the potatoes until just tender. Whizz the garlic and almonds to a fine paste in a small food processor or blender (or crush them in a mortar if you are feeling energetic). Transfer to a bowl and mix in the cayenne and paprika. Stir in the vinegar and olive oil, followed by the herbs, then season with a little salt. Pour over hot potatoes and serve.

Nutritional value per serving:
Calories: 323
Fats: 17.4g
Carbohydrates: 38g
Salt: 0.32g

baked potatoes with mozzarella, basil, & sun-blushed tomatoes

4 large, floury potatoes

8 garlic cloves

2 tablespoons olive oil

4 good handfuls of basil leaves, roughly chopped

4oz sun-blushed tomatoes, cut into small pieces

1⅓ cups (about 9oz) buffalo mozzarella, cut
    into ¼in dice

salt and freshly-ground black pepper

Preheat the oven to 350°F. Bake the potatoes until tender. Meanwhile, place the unpeeled garlic cloves in a baking pan, pour over the oil and roast in the oven for 25-30 minutes, until golden and caramelized. Remove the skins and mash the flesh coarsely in a bowl. Add the basil, mozzarella, and tomatoes and season lightly.

Make an incision or a cross in the center of each potato and open it up. Fill with the cheese and tomato mixture and return to the oven for 8-10 minutes, until the mozzarella is bubbling.

TIP

Baked garlic cloves are sweet and tender. Make more than you need and add the puree to mayonnaise, or pasta sauces.

Nutritional value per serving:

Calories: 472

Fats: 27.3g

Carbohydrates: 37g

Salt: 1.52g

roasted baby **carrots** with cumin

2 teaspoons cumin seeds

3 tablespoons olive oil

½ small garlic clove, crushed

1lb 10oz baby carrots, lightly scraped

2 tablespoons honey

juice and shredded rind of 1 orange

chopped mint, to garnish (optional)

Preheat the oven to 400°F. Heat a large ovenproof skillet over a moderate heat, add the cumin seeds and toast for 30 seconds to release their fragrance. Add the olive oil and garlic and mix well. Stir in the carrots and toss until they are sealed and lightly golden all over.

Add the honey and orange juice and rind and stir well to combine.

Transfer to the oven and cook for 8-10 minutes, until the carrots are glazed and tender and all the liquid has evaporated. Serve immediately, sprinkled with a little mint, if you like, which goes well with the spiced carrots.

Nutritional value per serving:

Calories: 168

Fats: 9.6g

Carbohydrates: 19g

Salt: 0.20g

red cabbage with dried fruits & juniper

7 cups red cabbage, core removed,
    finely shredded

1¼ cups red wine

⅔ cup port

5 tablespoons red wine vinegar

1 tablespoon brown sugar

2½ cups well-flavored chicken broth

5oz mixed ready-to-eat dried fruits, such as
    apricot, pear, fig, and apple, halved

12 juniper berries

2 tablespoons redcurrant jelly

salt and freshly-ground black pepper

Preheat the oven to 400°F. Place the shredded cabbage in a large ovenproof dish, pour over the red wine, port, and wine vinegar, then sprinkle over the sugar and season lightly.

Bring the broth to a boil, then pour it over the cabbage and add the dried fruit and juniper berries. Bring to a boil, cover with a tight-fitting lid, then transfer to the oven and braise for up to 1 hour or until the cabbage is very tender. If any liquid remains, uncover the pan and continue to cook until evaporated. Add the redcurrant jelly, mix well to form a glaze around the cabbage, then serve immediately.

How to shred red or white cabbage

Cut the cabbage into quarters and remove the hard center. Turn each slice onto its side and slice thinly lengthways.

Nutritional value per serving:

Calories: 233

Fats: 1g

Carbohydrates: 31g

Salt: 0.84g

SERVES 4

PREPARATION TIME: 15 MINUTES

COOKING TIME: 1 HOUR

balsamic-braised red cabbage with cranberries

7 cups red cabbage, cored and finely shredded
(see page 144)

1³/₄ cups red wine

5 tablespoons balsamic vinegar

1 tablespoon brown sugar

4¹/₂oz fresh or frozen cranberries

2 tablespoons cranberry jelly (or redcurrant jelly)

salt and freshly-ground black pepper

Preheat the oven to 400°F. Place the shredded cabbage in a large casserole, pour over the red wine and balsamic vinegar and place over a medium heat for 5 minutes. Sprinkle over the sugar and season lightly. Pour in 2¹/₂ cups of water and bring to a boil, then add the cranberries. Cover with a tight-fitting lid and transfer to the oven. Braise for 1 hour or until the cabbage is very tender. If any liquid remains, place the casserole on the hob and cook, uncovered, until it evaporates. Stir in the cranberry jelly, adjust the seasoning and serve immediately.

Nutritional value per serving:

Calories: 136

Fats: 0.5g

Carbohydrates: 15g

Salt: 0.31g

braised beetroot with shallots

4-6 (about 1lb) small to medium beetroot

²/₃ cup red wine

2 tablespoons red wine vinegar

2 tablespoons superfine sugar

1¼ cups well-flavored vegetable broth

9 small shallots, blanched and peeled

salt and freshly-ground black pepper

Preheat the oven to 375°F. Peel the beetroot carefully, retaining their shape, then cut them into slices ½in thick and set aside.

Mix the red wine, vinegar, sugar, and vegetable broth in a bowl. Arrange the beetroot and shallots in a single layer in an ovenproof dish. Pour over the red wine mixture and season with salt and pepper. Cover with aluminum foil or a tight-fitting lid and bake for about 1-1¼ hours or until the vegetables are tender. Serve immediately.

TIP

For a nice variation, top the beetroot with a spoonful of creamed horseradish before serving.

Nutritional value per serving:

Calories: 111

Fats: 0.3g

Carbohydrates: 19g

Salt: 0.71g

mediterranean-style fennel

12-16 baby fennel bulbs (or 4 ordinary fennel
   bulbs, cut into quarters)

4 tablespoons olive oil

4 garlic cloves, peeled

1 bay leaf

$1/3$ cup dry white wine

$1/3$ cup water

8 large scallions, cut into 2in lengths

4 ripe but firm plum tomatoes, skinned, pitted
   and cut into quarters (see page 90)

1 tablespoon chopped fresh oregano

$1/3$ cup meat broth

12 fresh purple basil leaves

a little lemon juice

salt and freshly-ground black pepper

Remove the fronds from the fennel and trim the bulbs. Heat the olive oil in a shallow saucepan, add the fennel and whole garlic cloves and sauté for 5 minutes. Add the bay leaf, white wine, and water and bring to a boil, then reduce the heat and simmer for 10 minutes, Add the scallions, cover the pan and cook for 15 minutes. Remove the lid, add the tomatoes, oregano, and broth and cook over a gentle heat for 5 minutes. Finally stir in the purple basil, add a squeeze of lemon juice and season with salt and pepper. Serve immediately.

Nutritional value per serving:

Calories: 161

Fats: 11.7g

Carbohydrates: 7g

Salt: 0.4g

stout-braised winter **vegetables**

2 tablespoons virgin olive oil

12oz small onions (about 1-1¼in in diameter),
   blanched and peeled

4 celery stalks, cut into 2in batons

2 garlic cloves, crushed

6 young carrots, scraped

²/₃ cup stout (or other dark beer)

¹/₃ cup tomato juice

³/₄ cup vegetable broth

1 tablespoon brown sugar

salt and freshly-ground black pepper

Heat the olive oil in a large saucepan, add the onions and celery and fry over a moderate heat until lightly golden, about 10-12 minutes. Add the garlic and cook for a couple of minutes, then stir in the carrots. Add the beer, tomato juice, vegetable broth, and sugar and bring to a boil. Cover the pan, reduce the heat and cook gently for about 10 minutes or until the vegetables are tender.

Arrange the vegetables in a serving dish, then season the sauce and pour it over them. It should be thick enough to glaze the vegetables; if necessary, boil it down a little first to thicken it.

Nutritional value per serving:

Calories: 133

Fats: 6g

Carbohydrates: 17g

Salt: 0.7g

baked **onions** with rosemary

4 large Spanish onions
2½ cups chicken broth (or vegetable broth)
4 branches of rosemary, roughly chopped
4 tablespoons virgin olive oil
½ stick chilled unsalted butter, diced
salt and freshly-ground black pepper

Preheat the oven to 400°F. Peel the onions, trim the top and bottom so they will sit upright, then cut them in half horizontally. Arrange in a flameproof baking dish, pour over the broth, then scatter over the chopped rosemary and season well. Pour over the olive oil, place in the oven and bake for about 50 minutes, basting the onions regularly with the broth.

Remove the onions from the oven and put them into an ovenproof serving dish. Put the baking dish over a medium heat and bring the cooking liquid to a boil, then remove from the heat and whisk in the butter, a little at a time. Pour the sauce back over the onions and return them to the oven for 15-20 minutes, until they have a wonderful shiny glaze and are very tender.

Nutritional value per serving:
Calories: 270
Fats: 21.8g
Carbohydrates: 16g
Salt: 0.76g

cornmeal with mushrooms & gorgonzola

4 tablespoons olive oil

6 shallots, finely chopped

2 garlic cloves, finely chopped

12 flat-cap mushrooms, sliced

8oz mixed wild mushrooms

2 sprigs of thyme, finely chopped

1 glass of white wine

1$\frac{1}{3}$ cups heavy cream

1 cup Gorgonzola, roughly cubed

1$\frac{1}{2}$ cups Parmesan cheese, grated

a handful of flat-leaf parsley, finely chopped

juice of $\frac{1}{2}$ lemon

1 packet (1lb 2oz) of cornmeal, cooked
according to packet instructions and
charbroiled

Put the olive oil in a large wide-bottomed saucepan set over a low heat, add the shallots and garlic, and cook gently until the shallots are softened. Turn the heat up to high and add all the mushrooms, both sliced and whole wild. Cook for 4-5 minutes, stirring occasionally. Add the thyme and cook for a further minute. Reduce the heat to moderate and cook for a further 5 minutes. Add the wine and reduce by two thirds. Add the cream and allow to boil, stirring constantly, until the sauce is reduced by one third, then turn the heat down to low.

Add the Gorgonzola, Parmesan, parsley, and lemon juice, stirring constantly until the cheeses have melted. Serve poured over grilled polenta.

How to cook and grill cornmeal

Make up the cornmeal according to the packet instructions and pour into a greased round pan. Leave until cold then cut into triangles. Heat a ridged broiler pan, oil each piece of cornmeal and fry until charbroiled.

Nutritional value per serving:

Calories: 809

Fats: 51.5g

Carbohydrates: 64g

Salt: 1.60g

desserts

raspberry crème brûlée

3 egg yolks

2 eggs

¼ cup sugar

1 cup milk

1 cup heavy cream

2 vanilla pods, split and seeds removed

½ cup mascarpone

1 cup raspberries, plus a few extra
    for decoration

½ cup superfine sugar

Preheat the oven to 250°F. Whisk the egg yolks and eggs in a bowl with the sugar until pale and creamy. Heat the milk and cream over gentle heat and slowly pour into the egg mixture. Strain through a fine strainer and then scrape in the vanilla seeds. While the mixture is still warm, add the mascarpone and mix well.

Place the raspberries in the bottom of four ramekins and pour in the custard. Place the ramekins in a baking dish as shown below. Place in the oven and cook for 30-40 minutes. Remove from the heat and allow to cool.

To finish, sprinkle each ramekin with a layer of superfine sugar and glaze under a broiler until the sugar caramelizes. Allow to cool, then decorate with a few fresh raspberries.

How to use a bain-marie

To make a bain-marie, half-fill a baking dish with water and place the ramekins inside. Check during the cooking to make sure the water doesn't boil dry.

Nutritional value per serving:

Calories: 702

Fats: 50.7g

Carbohydrates: 54g

Salt: 0.33g

poached pears in vanilla with fromage blanc sorbet

4 large, firm pears, peeled and cored, but left
    whole

mint sprigs, to decorate

Syrup

2$\frac{1}{3}$ cups superfine sugar

4 cups water

3 vanilla pods

peel of 1 orange

peel of 1 lemon

1 teaspoon rosewater

1 star anise

1 clove

Fromage blanc sorbet

2 cups water

3oz glucose

1oz trimouline (optional) – see TIP

4 tablespoons lemon juice

2 cups (1lb) fromage blanc or soft white cheese

Nutritional value per serving:

Calories: 775

Fats: 9g

Carbohydrates: 175g

Salt: 0.13g

Place all the syrup ingredients in a saucepan over low heat until the sugar is dissolved. When all the sugar has dissolved completely, boil for 30 minutes. Let it cool to 75°C.

Add the pears and cook for 30 minutes on a low heat until the syrup has reduced by half. Transfer the pears to a shallow dish and strain the syrup over them. Wash out the pan.

For the sorbet, place the water, glucose, trimouline (if using) and lemon juice in the pan and bring to a boil. Let the mixture cool and then add the fromage blanc. Process in an ice-cream machine for about 40 minutes or freeze in a plastic container, taking the sorbet out and whisking it at intervals to prevent the formation of over-large ice crystals.

To serve, arrange each pear in the center of a large plate and decorate with a mint sprig. Pour some syrup around the pear and serve with a scoop of sorbet.

TIP

Trimouline is a water/sugar spray that can be added to keep the sorbet soft when frozen. If you do not have access to trimouline, simply take the sorbet out of the freezer quarter of an hour before serving to allow it to soften.

sticky rice with **mango**

1 cup coconut milk

2 tablespoons granulated sugar

$1/2$ teaspoon salt

10oz Thai sticky rice, cooked and still warm

4 ripe mangoes

2 tablespoons coconut cream

Combine the coconut milk and sugar in a small saucepan and heat gently, stirring all the time, until the sugar has dissolved. Do not allow to boil.

Stir in the salt and warm, cooked, sticky rice and set aside.

Peel the mangoes and cut off the 2 outer 'cheeks' of each fruit, as close to the center pit as possible. Discard the pit. Slice each piece of fruit into 4 lengths.

Place a mound of sticky rice in the center of a serving dish and arrange the slices of mango around it. Pour the coconut cream over the sticky rice and serve warm or cold.

TIP

To cook 1lb sticky rice, cover in water and soak for at least 3 hours, preferably overnight. Drain and rinse thoroughly. Line the perforated part of a steamer with double thickness cheesecloth and place the rice on top. Bring the water in the bottom of the steamer to the boil and steam the rice over a moderate heat for 30 minutes.

COCONUT MILK AND CREAM.

Buy this in cans. The thin liquid that collects at the top of the tin (before it is shaken or stirred) is called coconut milk. After stirring or shaking, the thick liquid is called coconut cream. It's as simple as that!

Nutritional value per serving:

Calories: 469

Fats: 13.6g

Carbohydrates: 85g

Salt: 0.82g

SERVES 10

PREPARATION TIME: 10 MINUTES

COOKING TIME: 35 MINUTES

SETTING TIME: 4 HOURS

fresh blueberry & raspberry jelly with mint cream

1 cup fresh raspberries

1 cup fresh blueberries

Syrup

1 cup sugar

1 cup water

4 sprigs fresh mint

1 dessertspoon framboise or myrtille liqueur

1 tablespoon freshly squeezed lemon juice

3 rounded teaspoons gelatine

3 tablespoons water

Mint cream

15 mint leaves

1 tablespoon freshly squeezed lemon juice

3/4 cup cream

Line 10 ramekins or individual molds with plastic wrap and set aside.

Make a syrup by bringing sugar, water, and mint sprigs slowly to a boil. Simmer for a few minutes, allow to cool, add the liqueur and lemon juice.

Sponge the gelatine in the water in a small bowl or pint measure, then place the bowl in a pan of simmering water until the gelatine completely dissolves. Remove the mint leaves from the syrup, then pour the syrup onto the gelatine and add to the raspberries. Fill the lined molds. Put into the fridge and leave to set for 3-4 hours.

Meanwhile make the mint cream. Crush the mint leaves in a pestle and mortar with the lemon juice, add the cream and stir (the lemon juice will thicken the cream; if the cream becomes too thick add a little water).

Spread a little mint cream on a white plate, turn out a jelly and place in the center. Place mint leaves on the cream around the jelly. Decorate with a few perfect raspberries and blueberries. Serve chilled.

Nutritional value per serving:

Calories: 147

Fats: 3.5g

Carbohydrates: 27g

Salt: 0.05g

green gooseberry and elderflower **compote**

3-4 elderflower heads

2 cups sugar

2^1/$_2$ cups cold water

2lb green gooseberries, topped and tailed

Tie the elderflower heads in a little square of cheesecloth. Put into a stainless-steel saucepan, add the sugar and cover with cold water. Bring slowly to a boil and continue to boil for 2 minutes. Add the gooseberries and simmer just until the fruit bursts. It is essential to cook the fruit until it actually bursts, otherwise the compote will be too bitter. Allow to get cold. Serve in a pretty bowl and decorate with fresh elderflowers.

TIP

Make sure you pick your elderflower heads from areas where there is not too much passing traffic.

Nutritional value per serving:

Calories: 324

Fats: 0.6g

Carbohydrates: 83g

Salt: 0.03g

cherries flambés with geranium-scented mascarpone

1-2 lemon-scented geranium leaves

$2/3$ cup superfine sugar

$1^{1}/_{4}$ cups mascarpone

$1/2$ cup sour cream

2lb 4oz cherries, washed, dried, and pitted

2 tablespoons superfine sugar

juice of 1 lemon

4 tablespoons kirsch

A few days before you make this dessert place the clean, dry geranium leaves in a small container with the sugar. Cover and leave to stand so that the sugar becomes scented with the wonderful lemony flavor.

On the day of serving, remove and discard the geranium leaves and combine the sugar with the mascarpone and sour cream. Keep in the fridge until required.

Place the cherries into a large heavy skillet. Sprinkle over the sugar and lemon juice and cook over a low heat for 3-5 minutes until the sugar dissolves and the cherries are heated through.

Once the cherries are hot, have a long match at hand, tip in the kirsch, light with the match and stand well back!

Take the flaming pan to the table and serve from the pan, passing round the scented cream separately.

Nutritional value per serving:

Calories: 294

Fats: 17.3g

Carbohydrates: 30g

Salt: 0.12g

spiced **baked bananas** with honey and yogurt

4 large bananas, peeled and sliced lengthways

2 tablespoons butter

2 tablespoons fresh orange juice

pinch of ground cinnamon

pinch of ground cloves

2 cardamom pods

4 good teaspoons honey

4 tablespoons plain yogurt

Preheat the oven to 400°F.

Place the bananas in a lightly oiled ovenproof dish and spread the rest of the butter on each slice.

Mix together the fresh orange juice, the spices, and the honey and pour over the bananas. Cover with a lid or aluminum foil and bake in the oven for 20 minutes, until the bananas are soft. Serve hot with a spoonful of yogurt each.

Nutritional value per serving:

Calories: 191

Fats: 5.8g

Carbohydrates: 34g

Salt: 0.16g

index

acknowledgments

The publishers would like to thank the following authors for permission to use the recipes reproduced on the pages indicated: **Hugo Arnold**: 24, 32, 98, 110; **Darina Allen**: 16, 18, 26, 42, 66, 68, 120, 126, 166, 168; **Ed Baines**: 106, 124, 156; **Aliza Baron-Cohen, Adrian Mercuri and Louisa J Walters**: 62, 172; **Vatcharin Bhumichitr**: 22, 80, 164, **Conrad Gallagher**: 14, 20, 30, 34, 44, 48, 54, 56, 72, 74, 78, 82, 88, 94, 96, 100, 104, 118, 122, 124, 128, 130, 134, 136, 160, 162,; **Paul Gayler**: 28, 36, 46, 50, 52, 58, 60, 64, 76, 86, 90, 102, 108, 114, 116, 138, 140, 142, 144, 146, 148, 150, 152, 154; **Oded Schwartz**: 170; **Sarah Woodward**: 40, 84, 112.

The publishers would like to thank the following photographers for permission to use the images reproduced on the pages indicated: **Martin Brigdale**: 23, 81, 165; **Julie Dixon**: 171; **Gus Filgate**: 1, 2, 12, 15, 21, 31, 35, 37, 38, 41, 45, 49, 51, 55, 57, 61, 65, 70, 73, 75, 79, 83, 85, 89, 91, 92, 95, 97, 101, 103, 105, 107, 113, 119, 123, 125, 129, 131, 132, 135, 137, 138, 141, 145, 149, 151, 153, 157, 158, 161, 163; **Georgia Glynn Smith**: 29, 47, 53, 59, 77, 87, 109, 115, 117, 143, 147, 155; **Ray Main**: 5, 7, 9, 17, 19, 20, 25, 27, 33, 43, 67, 69, 72, 78, 90, 99, 102, 111, 116, 121, 122, 127, 167, 169; **Juliet Piddington**: 63, 173; **Jean-Luc Scotto**: 28, 30, 36, 60, 68, 108, 126, 144, 156, 160.